Selena Gomez

BY JAN BERNARD

Published by The Child's World®
1980 Lookout Drive • Mankato, MN 56003-1705
800-599-READ • www.childsworld.com

Acknowledgments
The Child's World®: Mary Berendes, Publishing Director
The Design Lab: Cover and interior design
Amnet: Cover and interior production
Red Line Editorial: Editorial direction

Photo credits
Featureflash/Shutterstock Images, cover, 1; Shutterstock
Images, 5; Michael Tran/FilmMagic/Getty Images, 7; LM Otero/
AP Images, 9; Paul Hawthorne/WireImage/Getty Images, 11;
DFree/Shutterstock Images, 13; Chris Pizzello/AP Images, 15;
Dimitrios Kambouris/WireImage/Getty Images, 17; Gaas/AP
Images, 19; Joe Seer/Shutterstock Images, 21, 27; Northfoto/
Shutterstock Images, 23; John Steel/Shutterstock Images, 24;
Randy Miramontez/Shutterstock Images, 29

Design elements
Sergey Shvedov/iStockphoto

ISBN 9781614732952
LCCN 2012933736

Printed in the United States of America
Mankato, MN
July 2012
PA02128

Table of Contents

CHAPTER 1

Big Dreams

Many kids dream of becoming famous some day. Some dream of being a famous movie star. Other kids dream of being a sports hero. But most have to wait until they are adults for those dreams to come true. Not Selena Gomez. Thanks to a big purple dinosaur, she was able to get her start before she turned ten.

Selena's first role was on *Barney & Friends* in 2001. It was a kids' television show featuring a happy talking and singing dinosaur named Barney. Selena's acting career took off a few years after that. She has acted on television and in movies. She performs her music on concert stages around the world. Selena also has a big heart. She loves helping people and animals in need. Selena had big dreams growing up in Texas. She had no idea how far those dreams would take her.

Selena Gomez got her start in acting at a young age.

CHAPTER 2

A Little Town in Texas

Selena Marie Gomez was born on July 22, 1992. She grew up in Grand Prairie, Texas. It is a few miles outside of Dallas. Her mom was only 16 when Selena was born. Her dad's family originally came from Mexico.

Selena's parents got divorced when she was five years old. Her family never had much money. Selena's grandmother often babysat for her. Her grandmother would read *The Wonderful*

Selena was named after a famous singer from Mexico, Selena Quintanilla-Perez. Selena grew up listening to her music.

Selena poses with her mom in 2009.

Wizard of Oz to Selena over and over. It is still one of Selena's favorite books. Selena's mom is remarried now, but Selena is still an only child.

CHAPTER 3

One Big Dinosaur

Selena's mom acted in local plays. Selena often tagged along to watch. Selena decided she wanted to act, too. The television show *Barney & Friends* had an **open casting call** in 2001. Selena's mom was not sure if it was a good idea. But Selena convinced her mom to let her try out.

Selena was one of 1,400 kids who showed up for the **audition**. Another girl waiting in line asked Selena if she would like to color together while they waited. That girl was Demi Lovato. Both got roles on *Barney & Friends*. They also both became close friends and famous actresses.

Selena loves pickles and whole lemons with salt. It is a taste she picked up growing up in Texas.

Selena got her acting start on
Barney & Friends.

CHAPTER 4

What Comes after Barney?

The kids on *Barney & Friends* needed to be of a certain age. After two years on the show, Selena became too old. She was dropped from the show in 2003. It was time to look for other acting jobs.

Selena got a small role in the movie *Spy Kids 3-D: Game Over* later that year. Then, in 2004, she was chosen to audition in the Disney Channel's first worldwide casting search. Selena was nervous. Even though she had been on *Barney & Friends*, she still had stage fright sometimes. Selena and her mom worked to overcome this. Her mom told her to just focus on her dream. Many actors tried out. But Selena won.

Kids watch *Spy Kids 3-D: Game Over* in New York.

Selena made two **pilots** for television shows. However, neither was put on television right away. She guest starred in two popular Disney Channel shows. They were *The Suite Life of Zack and Cody* and

Hannah Montana. Meanwhile, she got a small part in the television movie *Walker, Texas Ranger: Trial by Fire*.

Selena balanced her acting jobs with normal life. She went to middle school at home in Texas. Selena played on the basketball team there. She was also voted most friendly in sixth grade.

Selena took on many small roles while building her acting career.

CHAPTER 5

From *The Wizard of Oz* to *Wizards of Waverly Place*

Maybe Selena's love of *The Wonderful Wizard of Oz* was a sign of things to come. She got her big break in 2007. Selena was cast as Alex Russo on the new Disney Channel show *Wizards of Waverly Place*. She also sang the show's theme song. It was called "Everything Is Not What It Seems." The show has won many awards, including an Emmy for Outstanding Children's Program in 2009. Selena won the Teen Choice

Selena loves Converse shoes. In 2007 she said she had more than 20 pairs in various colors!

Selena and her *Wizards of Waverly Place* costars show off their Emmy Awards.

Award for Choice TV Actress, Comedy, in 2011. She also won the Kids' Choice blimp award from the Nickelodeon television network for Favorite TV Actress in 2009, 2010, and 2011.

Selena and her mom moved to Los Angeles, California, to film *Wizards of Waverly Place*. There, they shared an apartment with Demi and her mom. Selena said Los Angeles was like living in Oz. Many things were different than living at home in Texas. Once she went to a movie and asked for a pickle at the concession stand. That is something she often ordered in Texas. But she was told they did not sell that kind of thing in Los Angeles movie theaters. Selena said she missed being able to get pickles at the movie theater.

Selena and Demi Lovato have been close friends throughout their acting careers.

CHAPTER 6

More than Wizards

Selena's success on *Wizards of Waverly Place* helped her get other opportunities. In 2008, she did **voice-overs** for the movie *Horton Hears a Who!* Selena voiced all 90 of the Whoville mayor's daughters. She also starred in the movie *Another Cinderella Story* along with Demi. Selena sang three songs for the film's soundtrack. Things were looking good. *Forbes* magazine ranked her fifth on its "Eight Hot Kids to Watch" list that year.

Selena filmed *Princess Protection Program* in 2009 for the Disney Channel. Her good friend Demi was also in that movie. Their **duet** "One and the Same" was featured in the film.

Selena poses with singer Taylor Swift at the opening of *Another Cinderella Story*.

Selena then filmed *Wizards of Waverly Place: The Movie*. She also sang four songs for the soundtrack. The movie was about the Russo family's vacation in the Caribbean, so it was filmed in sunny Puerto Rico. It aired on the Disney Channel in 2009. A whopping 11.4 million people watched.

Selena loves animals. In Puerto Rico, she was saddened by the poor treatment of homeless dogs there. So Selena and some friends teamed up with DoSomething.org and went out to find homeless puppies on the beach. They cleaned them up and sent them to animal shelters for adoption. Selena already had four shelter-adopted dogs at the time. That did not stop her from adopting one more in Puerto Rico. She later adopted one more after that!

Selena has dated singer Nick Jonas and actor Taylor Lautner. However, her relationship with famous singer Justin Bieber has brought her the most attention. Selena refuses to talk badly about any ex-boyfriend.

Selena poses with her boyfriend Justin Bieber in 2011.

CHAPTER 7

The Beat Goes On

Selena continued to expand her music career in 2008. She signed a recording contract with Hollywood Records that year. She also formed a band called Selena Gomez & the Scene. Her first album was called *Kiss and Tell*. It came out in 2009. Next came *A Year Without Rain* in 2010.

Selena had a big year in 2010. She graduated from high school that year. She was homeschooled on set during high school because she was so busy working. Selena also starred as Beezus in the movie *Ramona and Beezus*.

Selena is a big basketball fan. Her favorite team is the San Antonio Spurs. She also enjoys her iPod, the television show *Gossip Girl*, and the band Paramore.

Selena *(center)* films *Monte Carlo* in 2010.

Selena sings while in Indianapolis, Indiana, in 2010.

In 2011, Selena released her third album, *When the Sun Goes Down*. Selena wrote the song "Beautifully Disturbed" about her own life. One of Selena's best friends is singer Taylor Swift. It was Taylor who suggested Selena write songs about her own life. That way they are real to her and to her fans.

That year she also starred in the movie *Monte Carlo*. Her single from the movie, "Who Says," went platinum. That meant it sold more than one million copies. The future looked very bright for the 19-year-old.

CHAPTER 8

Branching Out

Selena was already a popular actress and singer. In 2010, she also became a clothing designer. She worked with professional designers to develop a teen clothing line. It was called Dream Out Loud. The clothes were sold at Kmart stores. Selena wanted to show kids they could express their personalities through fashion without spending a lot of money.

Selena supports many **charities**. She was the youngest UNICEF **ambassador** in history.

When Selena was 16, she teamed up with Kermit the Frog for charity. They did a public service announcement together. It brought attention to the endangered amphibians around the world.

UNICEF stands for the United Nations Children's Fund. It is a group that helps provide children in need around the world with food, health care, and education. Kids who support UNICEF go trick-or-treating on Halloween. However, instead of candy, they collect money for the charity. That money supports kids in need all over the world. Selena went to Ghana in 2009 and Chile in 2011 to see the good work UNICEF was doing. She also worked with an insurance company to raise awareness about safe driving.

Selena attends a charity event in 2008 in Los Angeles, California.

CHAPTER 9

A Texas Girl at Heart

Selena's mother gave her good advice. She told Selena to always remember where she came from. Selena is a Texas girl at heart. Even though she lives in Los Angeles with her mom and stepfather, she tries to get back to Texas as often as she can. Her cousins, grandparents, and aunts and uncles are there. Selena also has many friends in Texas

When asked what it means to be a strong girl, Selena said self-confidence is important. "You can't think that you're not as good as anyone else. And I think it's important to be careful of what you do and say, and who you hang out with."

Even though she is a big star, Selena remembers where she came from.

whom she has known since kindergarten. She is a star with her feet on the ground, but with enough success to have her dreams firmly in the clouds.

GLOSSARY

ambassador (am-BAS-uh-dur): An ambassador represents a country or an organization. Selena is an ambassador for UNICEF.

audition (aw-DISH-uhn): An audition is a performance where an actor or actress tries out for a role. Selena went to an audition for *Barney & Friends.*

charities (CHAR-i-tees): Charities are organizations that provide money or assistance to those in need. Selena donates time and money to several charities.

duet (doo-ET): A duet is when two people perform a song. Selena and Demi Lovato recorded a duet for *Princess Protection Program.*

open casting call (OH-puhn KAST-ing kawl): An open casting call is when all actors are invited to try out for a part. Selena went to an open casting call for the show *Barney & Friends.*

pilots (PYE-luhts): Pilots are trial episodes of television shows. Selena acted in Disney Channel pilots.

voice-overs (vois OH-vurs): Voice-overs are when an actor plays an animated character by performing the character's voice offscreen. Selena did voice-overs for *Horton Hears a Who!*

FURTHER INFORMATION

BOOKS

Baum, L. Frank. *The Wonderful Wizard of Oz.* Jackson Hole, WY: Archeion Press, 2007.

Cleary, Beverly. *Beezus and Ramona.* New York: Harper Trophy, 2006.

Edwards, Posy. *Selena Gomez: Me & You: Star of Wizards of Waverly Place and More.* London: Orion Publishing Group, 2011.

Rutherford, Lucy. *Demi Lovato and Selena Gomez: The Complete Unofficial Story of the BFFs.* Toronto: ECW Press, 2009.

WEB SITES

Visit our Web site for links about Selena Gomez: **childsworld.com/links**

Note to Parents, Teachers, and Librarians: We routinely verify our Web links to make sure they are safe and active sites. So encourage your readers to check them out!

INDEX

ABOUT THE AUTHOR

Jan Bernard has been an elementary teacher in both Ohio and in Georgia, and has written curriculum for schools for over seven years. She also is the author of seven books. She lives in West Jefferson, Ohio, with her husband and their dog, Nigel. She has two sons.